SHOCKWAVE
SOCIAL STUDIES

Extreme Sports

Lynette Evans

children's press®

An imprint of Scholastic Inc.

NEW YORK • TORONTO • LONDON • AUCKLAND • SYDNEY
MEXICO CITY • NEW DELHI • HONG KONG
DANBURY, CONNECTICUT

Library of Congress Cataloging-in-Publication Data

Evans, Lynette.
  Extreme sports / by Lynette Evans.
      p. cm. -- (Shockwave)
  Includes index.
  ISBN-10: 0-531-17759-9 (lib. bdg.)
  ISBN-13: 978-0-531-17759-4 (lib. bdg.)
  ISBN-10: 0-531-15493-9 (pbk.)
  ISBN-13: 978-0-531-15493-9 (pbk.)

1. Extreme sports--Juvenile literature. I. Title.

  GV749.7.E93 2008
  796.04'6--dc22

2007019447

Published in 2008 by Children's Press, an imprint of Scholastic Inc.,
557 Broadway, New York, New York 10012
www.scholastic.com

11 12 13 14 15 16 17
10 9 8 7 6 5 4 3 2

Printed in China through Colorcraft Ltd., Hong Kong

Author: Lynette Evans
Educational Consultant: Ian Morrison
Editor: Lynette Evans
Designer: Anne Luo
Photo Researcher: Jamshed Mistry

Photographs by: AAP Image/AP/Reed Saxon (Shaun White, p. 23); © **Bossaball SL/**
www.bossaball.com (p. 26); **Digital Vision** (skyboarder, p. 9); **Getty Images** (p. 12; wakeboarder
and boat, p. 19; skater on grind rail, p. 23; BMX dirt jumpers, mountain boarder, pp. 24–25; stunt
pogo, p. 27); **Istockphoto/©Maria Bibikova** (p. 8); **Jeff Evans** (girls, p. 13); **Jennifer and Brian**
Lupton (pro and con teenagers, pp. 30–31); © **Simon Carter** (Tasmanian sea stack climb, p. 13);
Tranz/Corbis (cover, p. 1; pp. 5–7; pp. 10–11; pp. 14–18; Asian wakeboarder, p. 19; pp. 20–22;
BMX freestyle rider, p. 25; bungee jumping, p. 27; motorbike stunt, pp. 30–31); **Tranz/Rex Features**
(pp. 28–29)

All illustrations and other photographs © Weldon Owen Pty Ltd.

CONTENTS

accelerate (*ak SEL uh rate*) to gain speed

altimeter (*al TIM uh tur*) an instrument that measures air pressure and can be used to determine altitude

belay (*bee LAY*) to manage a safety rope for a climber

carabiner (*ka ruh BEE nur*) a metal ring with a spring ——— clip on one side, used in climbing to secure ropes

deploy (*dee PLOY*) to open a parachute by pulling on the ripcord

freestyle the individual and creative expression of a sport, such as biking, snowboarding, or skydiving, that incorporates stunts in an original way

gravity the force that pulls objects toward the center of the earth

· ·

For easy reference, see Wordmark on back flap.
For additional vocabulary, see Glossary on page 32.

Originally, *belay* was a sailing term. It meant "to coil rope around a pin and secure it."

This snowboarder uses specialized equipment, such as ice axes, rope, **carabiners**, and ice-climbing boots, to climb up a frozen waterfall.

An extreme sport is a sport that pushes boundaries. Sometimes the boundaries are physical. Extreme sports can test what heights, depths, speeds, and challenges the human body can endure. Sometimes the boundaries are all in the mind. Extreme sports can push the limits of fear. They are usually risky, even if they are practiced as safely as possible.

Gravity is a key factor in many extreme sports. Gravity is the force that pulls a skydiver to the earth. It pulls a snowboarder down a slope, and a climber to the ground.

People who take part in extreme sports are often seeking the chance to defy gravity, even for just a few moments.

Extreme sports are also called action sports, or adventure sports. Most of these sports require a great deal of energy, **stamina**, **agility**, and training. Some require specialized equipment. Many extreme sports attract a crowd of both competitors and spectators.

Performers in Project Bandaloop combine dance with rock climbing and other sports. Part of their goal is to teach people about their environment.

Having reliable, well-maintained equipment and safety gear is very important for any extreme sport. Safety gear might include:

Rope

Harness

Helmet

Life vest

Knee pads

Elbow pads

Chutes and Skyboards

No one can actually *make* you jump out of a plane and into thin air. Even with a packed parachute, or chute, on your back and the knowledge that you have a reserve parachute, jumping is one extreme leap of faith! Imagine jumping from a plane that's more than 10,000 feet above solid ground. The landscape passes in a blur below you. Once you leave the roaring plane, there is just you and your parachute, the sky, and gravity. And if there's one thing on this planet that you can count on, it's gravity. Gravity brings you down. It can bring you down fast!

Skydivers and skysurfers often **deploy** their parachutes at about 2,000 to 2,500 feet above the ground. They can **free fall** for about a minute before they must pull the ripcord. When the **canopy** opens, it slows the rush toward ground.

Gravity causes everything to **accelerate** toward the earth. However, falling objects are slowed by the force of air pushing against them. The fastest speed at which a skydiver can fall is known as terminal velocity. Most skydivers reach a terminal velocity of about 120 miles per hour before they must deploy the parachute.

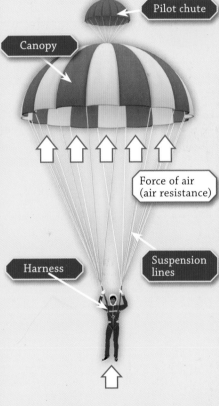

Pilot chute

Canopy

Force of air (air resistance)

Harness

Suspension lines

Skysurfers strap a skyboard to their feet. They spin and cartwheel through the air during free fall.

An **altimeter** is an instrument that keeps track of altitude. It is worn on the wrist and tells the skydiver when ground is approaching.

Altimeter

9

Barnstormers and BASE Jumpers

Sky-high tricks are not new. People have been tempted and thrilled by mid-air stunts ever since the first airplane flight in 1903. During the 1920s, daring pilots called barnstormers wowed crowds at airshows. Wing walkers were an important part of the early flight teams. They would climb onto the wings during flight and perform a range of **aerial** stunts. Parachute jumps were an exciting feature of barnstorming shows. Jumpers in those days sat on a trapeze-like swing beneath the airplane wing. Their parachutes opened as soon as they jumped.

BASE jumping also uses parachutes. It grew out of the sport of skydiving. Many people consider BASE jumping to be more of a daredevil stunt than a sport. BASE jumpers do not leap out of airplanes. They jump from fixed, earthbound objects, such as cliffs, buildings, towers, or bridges. The word BASE stands for Building, Antenna, Span, and Earth. Because BASE jumpers don't jump from a great height, their parachutes must open quickly.

Georgia Broadwick was a parachuting pioneer. People called Georgia "Tiny" because she was only four feet tall. Tiny made her first jump in 1908 at the age of fifteen. She went on to jump often in barnstorming shows. In 1914, Tiny made history when she made the world's first free-fall jump.

A BASE jumper descends from the Petronas Towers, in Malaysia.

parachute jumping

wing walking

BASE jumping

Mid-Air Thrills

free falling

barnstorming

trapeze swinging

11

Rock Climbing

Rock climbing is an exciting way for people to defy gravity and reach for new heights – literally! Rock climbing allows people to push the limits of their physical and mental abilities. Many people learn their first climbing moves in an indoor gym. Here, trained instructors, safety gear, and crash pads provide a safe setting. Climbers wear a harness and use a safety rope to climb a route up an indoor wall. Most climb with a **belay** partner. The belayer manages the rope and lowers the climber to the ground at the end of a climb.

Rock climbing can be scary. Sometimes climbers fall. Peeling off a wall or a rock face with nothing more than a rope between you and solid ground takes some getting used to. Climbers learn to trust the rope and the skills of their belay partner. They learn how to fall safely.

The rope is a climber's lifeline. Climbing ropes have some stretch, or give, but they are strong. Climbers tie a figure-eight knot to attach the rope to the harness.

Other climbing equipment includes:

Harness

Climbing shoes

Chalk bag

Helmet

Outdoor climbing offers a challenge for everyone, from the beginner to the extremely experienced climber. Only an expert would attempt climbing a column of rock more than 200 feet high, such as this one in Australia.

Ice Walls and Frozen Falls

Ice climbing is a sport that uses many of the same elements as rock climbing. But there is one unique addition — ice. Frozen water is not the most reliable substance. It is brittle, seriously slippery, and highly changeable. It has a tendency to melt when things heat up. When it first freezes, it is thin and difficult to climb. In extremely cold conditions, it shatters easily. What may be an easy climb one season can become a difficult climb the next.

Unique is in a class of words called absolutes. *Unique* means "one of a kind." So something can't be quite unique or very unique. Either it is or it isn't unique. Other absolutes include: *opposite, final, dead,* and *absolute*!

For many ice climbers, battling difficulty and danger is worthy payment for the breathtaking beauty of the earth's frozen places. Ice climbers set their sights high. Like rock climbers, they are determined to reach the top. They battle subzero temperatures, biting winds, and swiftly shifting skies to climb in mountainous areas. Ice-climbing equipment includes safety ropes, a climbing harness, **carabiners**, a helmet, and insulated clothing. **Crampons** on boots slice into the ice and allow a climber to ascend. An ice axe bites deep into the ice when swung. It gives the climber something solid to hold on to.

The X Games are a popular, annual action-sports event. There are both summer and winter X Games. Ice-climbing competitions take place during the Winter X Games. Ice cliffs, waterfalls, and towers are sculpted by workers just before a competition. Sometimes a super-cold chemical called liquid nitrogen is used to freeze the ice into walls that are thick and solid enough to climb.

Indoor ice-climbing wall

SHOCKER

Norway is a popular destination for ice climbers. It has frozen waterfalls, and huge ice cliffs as high as 900 feet!

The world's largest indoor ice-climbing wall is in Scotland. Climbers can learn basic skills indoors. They can also train and keep fit indoors before heading into the wild, white outdoors.

Running Rivers and Riding Rodeo

Kayaking is a sport that requires a high level of skill and stamina. Rivers can appear tame, but beneath even the most peaceful-looking surface, water may flow with powerful force. Arctic people used kayaks for transportation, fishing, and hunting more than 6,000 years ago. They made kayaks by stretching seal or caribou skins over a wooden or bone frame. From these beginnings came the kayak as we know it today. Most kayaks are now made of fiberglass or plastic. The kayaker sits in an opening called a cockpit. This is kept dry by a covering, or spray skirt. Should a kayak **capsize**, the paddler can use a technique known as an **Eskimo roll** to return the kayak to its upright position.

Some kayaks are designed for white-water paddling on rough rivers. Some are made for racing on river rapids. Some kayakers even run waterfalls. Rodeo kayaking is a sport that took off with the invention of short, plastic playboats. These are designed for surfing waves and performing tricks. Paddlers cartwheel, spin, and stand the boat on end.

Rodeo kayaker

Rivers are graded according to how difficult they are to travel on. The grades increase in danger from Grade 1 to Grade 6. Grade 1 rivers have little or no current and no big rocks. Grade 6 rivers are extremely dangerous. They have large drops over waterfalls and huge boulders. They are usually thought to be impossible to navigate, even by experts.

It is important always to wear a life vest when doing any form of kayaking. When paddling river rapids, a kayaker should also wear a helmet. Kayakers should always paddle with a partner.

An extreme kayaker descends a Grade 5 waterfall in Rock Creek, Washington.

If a kayak capsizes, the Eskimo roll maneuver (shown in the diagram below) allows a paddler to regain an upright position in seconds.

Waves and Wakes

Monster walls of water rise out of the sea off the coast of Hawaii. Some waves break as far as half a mile offshore. The speeding swells grow and curl. Then they crash against jagged coral and lava reefs. For some of the world's bravest and most skilled surfers, nature's wild, wet roller coaster provides the ultimate challenge and the greatest **adrenaline rush** of all.

Hawaii is the place where the sport of surfing began. When Captain Cook arrived there in 1778, an islander paddled out on a surfboard to greet him. The board was a large, heavy plank of wood. Today, surfboards are made of Styrofoam or fiberglass. They have fins to help with steering and a leash, or leg rope. Surfing competitions are held on big waves around the world.

> The first three or four sentences on this page are really descriptive. I think the author has done this to "paint a picture" of the wild and dangerous conditions.

Wakeboarding began when surfers were faced with flat seas and no chance to play. Wakeboarders hold onto a towrope attached to a powerboat. They jump waves that the boat makes in its **wake**. Like surfers, wakeboarders use a board with fins. They can perform spectacular stunts as they catch air.

Towrope

Board

Rubber boots

Wakeboarding

Most towropes are between 60 and 80 feet long. Rubber boots and bindings hold the wakeboarder's feet on the board.

Extreme wakeboarders use a towrope that is attached to a pole, called an extended pylon. This allows the wakeboarder to fly higher into the air in order to perform more complex tricks.

Wakeboarding competitions are popular events. Most wakeboarders compete on rivers and lakes. They earn points for the tricks they perform. Stunts include spins, flips, and **grabs**.

Stunts in the Snow

When it comes to extreme thrills, water seems to be a key ingredient, no matter what form it is in. Many people like water best in its frozen, powdery form. When the first snows of the winter season fall, skiers and snowboarders migrate to mountain playgrounds to test their skills on the slopes.

Many recently created words such as *snowboard* are compound words. *Freestyle* and *backcountry* are other examples of recently created compound words.

Some snowboarders ride up mountains on chairlifts. Some speed to the summit in a helicopter. Some hike into the **backcountry**. Once there, it's time to let gravity do its work. Snowboarders can carve their way down the slopes at high speeds. **Freestyle** snowboarders jump bumps, called moguls, and perform midair spins and stunts. Many ski areas have ramps and **half-pipes** for freestylers to practice their tricks on.

Snowboarding began in 1965. A man named Sherman Poppen saw that his little girl was trying to stand up on her sled as she went down a snowy hill. He went into his garage and screwed two children's skis together. He had made his daughter the first "snowboard." When the other kids saw what he had made, they all wanted one. Poppen called his invention a "snurfer." Snowboarding has come a long way since then. Boards are stable and easy to control once the basic techniques are learned. People young and old have taken up the sport.

Boards and Blades

Ramps and half-pipes increase the gravity factor in a number of action sports. For skateboarders and in-line skaters, racing down a vertical ramp provides the speed and **momentum** they need to perform highly skilled moves. Skaters wear helmets, knee and elbow pads, and sometimes wrist guards for safety. Skaters can jump more than ten feet into the air from the steepest ramps. These are often specially constructed for big-air events, such as the X Games and the Gravity Games. During these events, action-sports athletes enjoy thrills and endure spills to entertain crowds and compete for prizes.

Skateparks are the safest places to learn skating techniques. As well as having ramps and bowls to ride, skateparks have features of the urban environment. These include stairs, rails, curbs, and ledges. Skaters use these objects to do **grinds**, grabs, and other tricks.

Aggressive In-line

In-line skating is one of the fastest-growing sports in the world. Aggressive in-line is a form of the sport in which skaters do tricks and stunts in skateparks.

The grind is the basic move from which most other tricks are done. Aggressive skaters get air when they jump on and off a grind rail. The more air they get, the more spectacular the spins, flips, and grabs they can do.

Shaun White is known as "The Flying Tomato" because of his bright red hair. He won gold in the men's Skateboard Vert event at the 2007 Summer X Games.

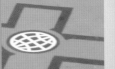

Grind rail

23

Dirt and Downhill

Some of the rockiest and most radical rides happen on mountain slopes. Twisting trails and dirt drop-offs provide **technical** challenges and heart-pumping thrills for mountain bikers who enjoy downhill racing. Extreme downhill racers ride at high speeds. They continue to pedal aggressively even down the steepest slopes. Full-body armor, gloves, pads, and full-face helmets help keep riders safe in the event of a **wipeout**. Their bikes are rugged and usually heavy for added **traction**. The tires are chunky.

Some bikers prefer tricks and style to speed. **BMX** dirt jumpers race around dirt or mud tracks with jumps and banked turns called **berms**. These give bikers the lift they need to perform aerial tricks as they race around the track.

Some freestyle BMX riders have become extremely skilled at their sport. They can pull off difficult high-speed, high-altitude acrobatics with their bikes. These aerial tricks have little to do with luck. Riders have been training hard and practicing their skills for a very long time. They have learned how to jump and land safely in order to minimize the risk of injury.

Bike Safety
- body armor (gloves, pads, helmets)
- well-constructed bikes
- experience (landing safely)
- training and practicing hard

Mountain boarders race down rocky mountain slopes during the summer season. They ride on all-terrain boards with chunky, rugged tires. Helmets and other safety gear help protect mountain boarders during their descent.

25

Bounce and Smash!

Imagine a sport that combines elements of beach volleyball, soccer, break dancing, and acrobatics with lively music that follows the ups and downs of the game! A bossaball court is made up of trampolines and inflatables. It is divided by a net. There are three to five players on each team. Players can use any part of the body to hit the ball. One point is scored when players on the inflatables ground the ball on the opponent's side of the court. However, the trampoline allows jumpers to gain height for a three-point smash. In some bossaball matches, **samba** referees use a whistle, a microphone, a soundtrack, and percussion instruments as they referee this high-energy game.

The Zambezi River drops suddenly into a deep, narrow gorge at the Victoria Falls in Africa. This bungee jumper gets an aerial view.

Bungee Jumping

Bungee jumpers climb into a body harness with a strong, elastic cord. The cord is secured to a jump platform on a bridge or a tower. Then they jump! The bungee cord stretches as it absorbs the energy of the fall. At the end of the fall, the jumper flies upward and continues to bounce up and down until all the energy from the fall is used.

Stunt pogo is another very bouncy sport that is growing in popularity. People perform a variety of stunts and tricks on their pogo sticks!

All Steamed Up

Some sports are thought of as **fringe** sports. They do not have a lengthy history and tradition. They do not attract large numbers of participants. They may not have the easily measurable results that are needed for competitive sports. Some people question whether these activities are sports at all.

Perhaps one of the most hotly debated is the sport of extreme ironing. Is this a joke, or do extreme ironers tackle their chosen sport with as much passion and **dedication** as any other athlete? Extreme ironing is a bizarre sport that combines the challenge of an exciting outdoor adventure with tidy, well-pressed clothing. Extreme ironers have been known to climb rock faces, hike or bike through forests, kayak river rapids, ski mountain slopes, and even scuba dive in order to reach some of the planet's most remote locations. Either on the way or at the destination, they set up an ironing board. Then they press a few items of clothing using a sturdy, battery-powered steam iron!

When I first read "extreme ironing," I thought I had it wrong. So I reread the sentence just to check. I did have it right! I guess I just didn't expect ironing to be a sport. Sometimes it's good to check, just to confirm you've got the right idea.

Mountaintop ironing

Underwater ironing

Humble Beginnings

The sport of extreme ironing began in 1997. A man named Phil Shaw came home from his job at a knitwear factory in England. At home, a mountain of creased laundry was waiting to be ironed. Shaw decided he would rather be rock climbing, but he dragged his ironing board out into the backyard. He got a long extension cord and began to iron. Since then, Shaw combines a bit of ironing with whatever extreme sport he is into. His nickname is "Steam"!

SHOCKER

An extreme ironer once cut an iron-shaped hole in a frozen lake in Wisconsin and dove in. However, when he surfaced with his freshly pressed shirt, it froze!

For Real or for Ridicule?

The first Extreme Ironing World Championship was held in Germany in 2002. Eighty teams from ten countries competed on an obstacle course laid out in the shape of an iron. The contestants could earn up to 120 points. The quality of their ironing counted for 60, their style counted for 40, and their speed counted for 20.

...cent times, media coverage of extreme-sports events has made the sports accessible to large numbers of people. These sports are growing quickly in popularity. Many people may not be able to participate in the events themselves. But they can get a taste of the action by being part of the crowd or by turning on the TV. During events such as the X Games, fans roar for spectacular stunts and wild moves. They hunger to see tricks that have never been done before.

WHAT DO YOU THINK?

Do you think there should be pressure for a sport to be more and more extreme?

PRO

I think competition is healthy. If athletes train hard enough to accomplish difficult techniques, they should get the rewards and recognition they deserve. It is encouraging to see what the human body can achieve. We shouldn't put a limit on how far extreme sports can go.

Competitors hurtle toward the ground from heart-stopping heights. They twist and flip in a breathtaking combination of airborne stunts. The most extreme tricks often earn the most applause and fattest rewards. However, the pressure to accomplish increasingly dramatic feats can cause a sport to become dangerous. The risks threaten to outweigh the thrills, and the concept of "extreme" is getting a negative reputation as reckless and foolish.

CON

I think it is irresponsible to try increasingly dangerous feats just so a sport can be considered extreme. Many young people try to imitate their sports heroes. As role models, these athletes should also promote safety in sports.

Go to **www.ducksters.com/sports/extreme.php** to learn more about extreme sports.

31

adrenaline rush the ready-for-action feeling produced by a hormone in the body called adrenaline

aerial (*AIR ee uhl*) having to do with the air

agility the ability to move quickly and easily

backcountry a rural region with few inhabitants

berm a narrow ledge or shelf along the top or bottom of a slope

BMX short for bicycle motorcross

canopy the part of a parachute that opens up and fills with air

capsize to overturn in the water

crampon a spiked iron plate worn on boots or shoes for aid in climbing or to prevent slipping on ice or snow

dedication (*ded uh KAY shun*) commitment and devotion to something

Eskimo roll a complete rollover in kayaking, from upright to upside down to upright

free fall to fall in midair before opening a parachute

fringe secondary or "on the edge" of usual practice

grab to take hold of either or both ends of a board or skates with one or both hands

grind to ride a skateboard along an obstacle, such as a handrail or the edge of a step

half-pipe a half-moon-shaped ramp used by snowboarders, skateboarders, and skaters to provide a takeoff for a jump

momentum the force or speed that an object has when it is moving

samba a lively and rhythmic Brazilian dance of African origin

stamina (*STAM uh nuh*) the fitness and strength to do something for a long time

technical having to do with skill

traction (*TRAK shuhn*) the gripping power that keeps something from slipping on a surface

wake the trail of ripples in the water left by a moving object

wipeout a fall